D0506979

HOW TO FEEL GREAT
ABOUT YOURSELF AND YOUR LIFE

HOW TO FEEL GREAT
ABOUT YOURSELF AND YOUR LIFE

A Step-By-Step Guide To Positive Thinking

Martin English

American Management Association

This book is available at a special
discount when ordered in bulk quantities.
For information, contact Special Sales Department,
AMACOM, a division of American Management Association,
135 West 50th Street, New York, NY 10020.

Library of Congress Cataloging-in-Publication Data

English, Martin.
    How to feel great about yourself and your life / Martin English.
        p. cm.
    ISBN 0-8144-7790-9
    1. Success in business--Psychological aspects.   2. Attitude
(Psychology).   3. Optimism.   4. Self-perception.   5. Personality and
situation.   I. Title.
HF5386.E55   1991
650.1-- dc20   91-58133
                                                                        CIP

©1992 AMACOM, a division of
American Management Association, New York.
All rights reserved.
Printed in the United States of America.

This publication may not be reproduced,
stored in a retrieval system,
or transmitted in whole or in part,
in any form or by any means, electronic,
mechanical, photocopying, recording, or otherwise,
without the prior written permission of AMACOM,
a division of American Management Association,
135 West 50th Street, New York, NY 10020.

Printing number

10 9 8 7

CONTENTS

ACKNOWLEDGMENTS

There are many people who have played a part, directly or indirectly, in the creation of this book. I want to acknowledge the tremendous influence of Norman Vincent Peale, a true pioneer in the realm of positive thinking and self-help. I also want to thank authors Shad Helmstetter and Denis Waitley for their inspiration and innovative approaches to self-management and personal success. And finally I want to thank my mother Carolyn whose gentle, caring attitude and relentless optimism pulled me through some dark times and helped shape my outlook on life.

HOW TO FEEL GREAT
ABOUT YOURSELF AND YOUR LIFE

EXAMINING YOUR ATTITUDE

What's your attitude right now? Would you say your attitude is good, bad, indifferent? Have you had this same outlook all day? Or did you have a different attitude when you woke up this morning? If so, why did your attitude change? More importantly, what exactly *is* "an attitude"?

ATTITUDE DEFINED

An attitude is the way an individual chooses to respond to all the stimuli encountered in daily life. Every one has an attitude *every* waking hour of *every* day. But most people seldom stop to think about or adjust their attitude until it reaches an extreme.

For instance, you are on your way to work and encounter highway construction which causes you to take a detour. How you *respond* to that particular situation is your attitude. You might begin to worry that the detour will make you late for work. You might curse your fate and grind your teeth all the way to the office. You might unknowingly allow that morning occurrence to affect your attitude for the rest of the day. Or you could choose a more positive response. You could realize that no amount of cursing or grinding will get you to work any faster. You might even take the time to observe the part of town your detour takes you through for any points of interest.

Successful attitude management is simply *being more aware of your attitude on a day-to-day basis and the times it changes.* An attitude is like the skin on a chameleon. It will always have it. But it can change the color of its skin at will. As human beings we will always have an attitude; but like the chameleon, it's very important to realize *we can change our attitude at will.* It's that ability to alter our attitude that will be explored in the pages to come.

A positive attitude is not only pleasant and productive for yourself; it causes others to respond favorably to you. Conversely, a negative attitude can lead to failure and discontent, causing others to avoid you. It's essential that we recognize the differences in our attitudes and how to affect them. In his book *The Joy of Working*, bestselling author Denis Waitley retells an Edward Pulling story which exemplifies polar attitudes. "Back in the Middle Ages, a dispatcher went out to determine how laborers felt about their work. He went to a building site in France. He approached the first worker and asked, 'What are you doing?' 'What, are you blind?' the worker snapped back. 'I'm cutting these impossible boulders with primitive tools and putting them together the way the boss tells me...it's back-breaking work, and it's boring me to death!' The dispatcher quickly backed off and retreated to a second worker. He asked the same question: 'What are you doing?' The worker replied, 'I'm shaping these boulders into usable forms, which are then assembled according to the architect's plans. It's hard work...but I earn five francs a week...It's a job. Could be worse.' The dispatcher went on to a third worker. 'And what are you doing?' he asked. 'Why, can't you see?' said the worker as he lifted his arm to the sky. 'I'm building a cathedral!' "

Attitude is a mind-set. It is a willful harnessing of your moods and emotions. Having a positive attitude means being able to focus on and accentuate positive events. It's the ability to recover when problems arise, or to salvage something good out of negative events. Sometimes having a positive attitude is as simple as wearing a genuine, heartfelt smile.

On the other hand, having a negative attitude means one dwells on problems instead of solutions. A negative outlook encourages worry and anxiety by lowering expectations and inviting failure. People with negative attitudes often complain and express their doubts unnecessarily. Often they alienate and "turn off" others because of their negative mind sets. Most people find themselves consciously or unconsciously avoiding individuals like these.

GETTING STARTED

What is your general attitude? What would you say is the tone of your collective thoughts and feelings each day? On the average where would you place yourself on the scale below?

HOW I SEE MYSELF

Positive   Indifferent   Negative

Would co-workers and friends characterize you as a person with a positive or negative attitude? How would they assess the manner in which you normally express yourself? Where would *they* place you on the scale?

HOW OTHERS SEE ME

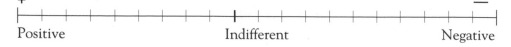

Positive   Indifferent   Negative

In order to better understand how your attitude fluctuates daily and the factors that affect it, why not examine the times during each day when you realize your attitude has changed? For the next three days, use the Three-Day Attitude-Tracking Chart to track your attitude. While completing it, feel free to proceed with the rest of this book since the following chapters will help you interpret it. You will want to use different color pens or different style lines to differentiate one day from the next. Once your chart is complete, look for similarities between the days. If you find any, circle the times of the day for those similarities that were positive, put a triangle around indifferent times, and draw a box around the times for those that were negative.

THREE-DAY ATTITUDE-TRACKING CHART

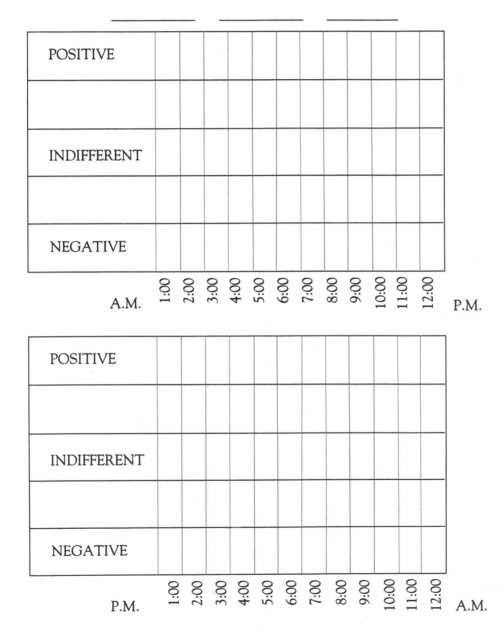

Then in the space provided below, record the time, the attitude, and the factors that may have affected the attitude.

POSITIVE

Time		Possible causal factors
_____:_____	A.M. P.M.	_____
_____:_____	A.M. P.M.	_____
_____:_____	A.M. P.M.	_____
_____:_____	A.M. P.M.	_____
_____:_____	A.M. P.M.	_____

NEGATIVE

Time		Possible causal factors
_____:_____	A.M. P.M.	_____
_____:_____	A.M. P.M.	_____
_____:_____	A.M. P.M.	_____
_____:_____	A.M. P.M.	_____
_____:_____	A.M. P.M.	_____

This exercise will help you discover your attitude patterns and understand what affects their changes. This knowledge will prove to be invaluable in creating and maintaining a positive outlook on your life.

In the following pages, we'll discuss how your attitude affects you, how you are affected by the attitudes of others, specific strategies to maintain a positive mind set every day, effective goal setting, and communication techniques that will ensure productive relationships with others and minimize the negative effects of misunderstandings. We'll also outline specific actions you can use to take control of your life, conquer your fears, and become a confident, productive force in any team or group.

However, before you proceed, it's important that you take a moment to set goals. In order to implement any changes in your life you must set specific goals for yourself. Exactly what do you hope to accomplish? How do you want to respond to daily situations? What effects do you want your attitude to have on your behavior? How would you like your attitude to affect those around you? Once you have answered these questions specifically for yourself, you'll be ready to start on the road to self-improvement.

ONE

WHAT'S YOUR ATTITUDE?

ATTITUDE AND YOU

1

IT ALL BEGINS WITH YOU

You can't be happy about life, your surroundings, and others if you're not happy with yourself. Happiness and positive attitude start at home, in your heart and mind. What you think and how you feel inside will inform every other aspect of your life. Unfortunately, according to Shad Helmstetter, Ph.D. and author of the best seller, *What to Say When You Talk to Yourself*, thinking positively is not always an easy task. Dr. Helmstetter explains "...that as much as seventy-seven percent of everything we think is negative, counterproductive, and works against us." That's why it's so important to begin teaching yourself to think positively. You must begin to improve your self-perception before setting your sights on any other facet of your life.

OUR INNER MONOLOGUE

To enhance the way you perceive yourself, Dr. Helmstetter has created a technique he calls "self-talk." This method of improving your attitude is based on his theory that, "The brain simply believes what you tell it most." In other words, "You are what you think." Because of this constant "inner monologue," if you speak to yourself in an affirming, positive manner you'll improve your self-perception and attitude. If your inner monologue is predominantly negative, your attitude will suffer.

Examples of negative inner monologues include:
This just isn't my day.
Oh, what's the use!
I'm not very creative.
Why do things like that always happen to me?
I hate my work.
I never seem to get anything done anymore.
That's just my luck!
That's typical!

I'm getting old.
If I just had a little more time...
If I just had a little more money...
I'm not a morning person.
I'm losing my mind!
I don't have the "guts."
I always stick my foot in my mouth!

Examples of positive inner monologues include:
I can do that easily.
That's no problem.
I am not a victim.
I am in control of this situation.
I have what it takes.
You can trust me.
I feel good about that.
I deserve the best.
I am successful.
I've got lots of energy.
I'm positive.

Listen to your inner monologue. What do you say to yourself every day? Are you constantly putting yourself down? Do you ever compliment yourself? If what you say to yourself is predominantly negative, it's time for a change.

TUNING YOURSELF

In order to improve your self-image and feel successful, you have to change and control your inner monologue. It's important to eliminate the negative phrases floating around in your mind and break the habit of attacking yourself with them. In this book *Being The Best*, Denis Waitley remarks, "The truth is you don't break a bad habit; you replace it with a good one." Instead of telling yourself what you *can't* do or are *not* capable of doing, you should be congratulating yourself on the things you *can do*. It's not an easy task, but you can accomplish it with conscious effort.

The bad news is the fact that up to 75 percent of our negative thoughts are unconscious. Our society has introduced so many don'ts, shouldn'ts, and can'ts into our minds that negative phrases are much more natural and accessible to us. The good news is that, like a piano, our minds can be tuned. Good pianos need frequent maintenance to avoid falling out of tune. The same is true of our minds. Neglect will allow negative thoughts to inject sour notes and discord into our lives. With hard work and conscious effort, we can tune our subconscious minds to a new inner monologue. We can create an inner monologue that is positive and affirming, one that will constantly reassure us of our abilities and worth.

The first step is to write down a *list of positive, personal phrases for your new inner monologue* in the following space. Be sure to use reinforcing words like "I can," "I should," "I will," "I want to," "I love to," and "I have." Be specific about your own qualities and abilities.

POSITIVE INNER-MONOLOGUE PHRASES

1._____

2._____

3._____

4._____

5._____

6._____

7._____

8._____

9._____

10._____

Once you have completed the list, read it aloud to yourself at least three times a day. Remember, your mind has had many years of negative programming causing it to fall out of tune. So, it's going to take some time to replace the old inner monologue with the new one. Repetition is the key.

The next step in tuning yourself is to begin *injecting positive words and phrases into your daily speech.* Strive consciously to use encouraging vocabulary as much as possible. Avoid the old habit of using negative words and phrases whenever you can. If your mind is constantly refreshed with positive vocabulary, tuning yourself will be considerably less difficult.

Finally, develop a support group whose members are warm, positive people. Spend more time with people who really care about you. None of us are capable of making it through life on our own. We all need the help, feedback, and support of others. A caring group of friends can help you understand your attitude and support you as you tune your inner monologue.

- THE CHAPTER IN BRIEF -

*Happiness and positive attitude begin with YOU.
*Your daily inner monologue directly affects your attitude.
*Tuning your inner monologue is essential for a positive attitude.
*List positive phrases for your new inner monologue.
*Inject positive vocabulary into your daily speech.
*Develop a support group.

YOUR ATTITUDE AND OTHERS'

2

How does your attitude affect your life? With careful self-examination you should be able to articulate precisely what facets of your life *influence* and are *influenced by* your attitude.

HOW OTHERS AFFECT YOUR ATTITUDE

How would you characterize the people in your life? Have you ever thought about the impact their attitudes have on you? In the blanks below, list your closest family members, co-workers, and friends. In the center column, identify each person's general attitude by circling (-) for negative, (o) for neutral and (+) for positive. Then, in the right column, how each of them affects you.

PERSON	GENERAL ATTITUDE	AFFECT ON ME
1._____	- / + / o	_____
2._____	- / + / o	_____
3._____	- / + / o	_____
4._____	- / + / o	_____
5._____	- / + / o	_____
6._____	- / + / o	_____
7._____	- / + / o	_____
8._____	- / + / o	_____
9._____	- / + / o	_____
10._____	- / + / o	_____

Were you surprised at any of the assessments you made? Is there a family member who always seems to cheer you up? Do you have a co-worker whose attitude seems to pull you down?

Many times the people who we think have a positive affect on our attitude, surprise us when we actually stop and analyze their words and actions. Consider those people who seem upbeat and positive but can never quite bring themselves to offer a compliment or be positive and encouraging to anyone. Or how about someone who always has an insult or verbal cut handy in conversation. Often the insult is laughed off as being clever banter or a witticism. Unfortunately, many of those insults hit their mark and really hurt those at whom they are directed. People whose egos have been damaged by these flippant remarks seldom, if ever, admit to the culprit that they were truly hurt by them. Through the media, our society has even popularized the type of person who has a quick, scathing wit capable of verbally damaging another.

Our society has made the victims of insults feel like they are weak or thin-skinned if they "allow" themselves to be offended. However, as Eleanor Roosevelt once said, *"Remember, no one can make you feel inferior without your consent."* You have the ultimate control over how the comments of another will affect your attitude.

However, you <u>cannot</u> <u>control</u> the attitudes and reactions of others. As with any major life change, only *they* can do that. But, you can try a direct approach with a friend or relative who you think might respond positively to constructive feedback. Explain how their words, actions, and attitude make you feel. In most cases, they probably don't realize the impact their attitude has had.

If you <u>don't</u> feel comfortable talking about your feelings, protect yourself by mentally preparing before spending time with that person again. For instance, begin with a positive attitude and tell yourself that you're not going to give that person the power to change it. Before spending time with them, think of several pleasant conversation starters. Take control of the conversation and lead that person toward positive subjects. Compliment the person in some way. Sometimes a simple, unsolicited compliment can alter a negative attitude. Finally, if the conversation begins to grow negative and you can't seem to change the subject, then politely excuse yourself and tell them you need to go. Don't allow a chance — or intended — encounter alter your frame of mind.

ATTITUDE AND FRIENDSHIP

No one enjoys spending time with people who are constantly complaining and pointing out the negative side of situations. Who wants to be with someone who seems joyless and filled with pessimism? Life is tough enough without constantly having to take on the problems and negativism of others.

Think about those people with whom you enjoy spending time. Would you characterize them as positive or negative? Most of your closest friends are probably positive; otherwise you wouldn't enjoy their company as much.

Attitude is *everything* in personal relationships. People can't always choose their co-workers, but *everyone* can choose their own friends. At work, you can be judged by your skills, but with friends you are judged only by your attitude and how you approach the relationship. How do your friends perceive you? What would they say is your general attitude toward them? How do you perceive yourself?

PERSONAL RELATIONSHIP ATTITUDE QUIZ

Please rate your attitude from 1—10 as it pertains to your personal relationships. Circle the number that best represents your attitude, keeping in mind that a number 1 means you strongly disagree and a number 10 means you strongly agree with the statement. Answer as quickly and candidly as possible.

		DISAGREE		AGREE
1.	I often argue with my spouse.		1 2 3 4 5 6 7 8 9 10	
2.	I often argue with my close friends.		1 2 3 4 5 6 7 8 9 10	
3.	I'm verbally critical when my friends make "stupid" mistakes.		1 2 3 4 5 6 7 8 9 10	
4.	I enjoy ribbing or cutting down my friends.		1 2 3 4 5 6 7 8 9 10	
5.	I laugh when I hear a really good insult.		1 2 3 4 5 6 7 8 9 10	
6.	I seldom compliment my spouse.		1 2 3 4 5 6 7 8 9 10	
7.	I seldom compliment my close friends.		1 2 3 4 5 6 7 8 9 10	
8.	I have trouble making new friends.		1 2 3 4 5 6 7 8 9 10	
9.	If asked, I could list more faults than virtues for my spouse or close friends.		1 2 3 4 5 6 7 8 9 10	
10.	When someone wrongs me, I often hold a grudge.		1 2 3 4 5 6 7 8 9 10	
11.	I feel uncomfortable and embarrassed when giving gifts to family and friends.		1 2 3 4 5 6 7 8 9 10	
12.	I feel uncomfortable and embarrassed when friends compliment me.		1 2 3 4 5 6 7 8 9 10	

Now add up your score. If you scored 50 or less, you have a good attitude when dealing with personal relationships. If you scored between 50 and 70, your attitude may need some modification. If you scored between 70 and 90, some major adjustments are necessary. If you scored over 90, you definitely need to change your attitude when dealing with your family and friends.

With an open, positive attitude you can significantly influence the way others perceive you. Your attitude is an integral part of your personality. Are you sending the right messages to others with your attitude?

Think about how others perceive you. In the spaces below, list words you think others would use to describe you.

People would describe me as:

_____   _____   _____

_____   _____   _____

_____   _____   _____

How would you prefer other people to perceive you? Are you reflecting who you really are? Do your actions, words, and facial expressions accurately convey your inner thoughts and feelings? Or do people get the wrong impression from your attitude? For example: Do people frequently think you're in a bad mood when you're not? Everyone has faults and undesirable aspects to their personalities. Your ultimate goal should be to show the positive sides of your personality. This doesn't mean that you need to act nice and full of joy with your friends all the time. Friends need and want to be involved in your life—even when times are tough and you're troubled. However, if your mood is constantly negative, your friends will begin to feel overburdened by it. They will tire of hearing about your problems and will have a distorted view of you. As we've mentioned before, nobody wants to be around someone who is always down or depressed.

Now that you've listed how you think others would describe you and we've discussed the affects your attitude has on others, refer back to the list of family, co-workers, and friends and their attitudes that you made earlier in this chapter. Choose the person you feel has the most positive attitude and write his or her name in the "positive person" blank. Next, choose the person you feel has the most negative attitude and write his or her name in the "negative person" blank. In the column of blanks beneath each name, list words that describe that person's attitude and personality. Use only single-word descriptions: adjectives, nouns, verbs, or even the names of characters from books and movies, whatever you think is appropriate. Avoid over-analyzing the individual. Simply list the first qualities that come to mind.

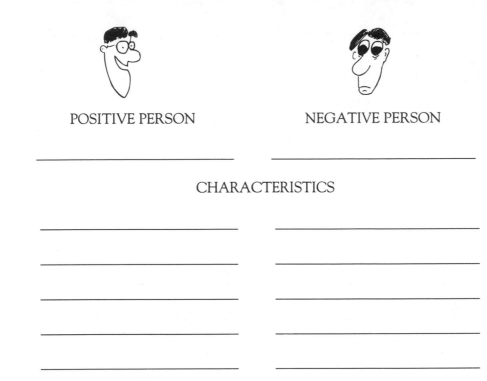

POSITIVE PERSON   NEGATIVE PERSON

_____   _____

CHARACTERISTICS

_____   _____

_____   _____

_____   _____

_____   _____

_____   _____

Now consider the types of words you've written for each person. What kinds of words did you use to describe the positive person? Did you list words like fun, pleasant, successful, winner, kind, caring, active, warm, friendly, happy? Now look at the words you listed in the negative person's column. Did you find yourself writing words like depressing, angry, tired, jumpy, nervous, worrier, loser, boring, offensive? Is that a description of a person you'd like to meet and spend time with? If not, perhaps you need to evaluate your relationship with that person.

ATTITUDE IN THE WORKPLACE

In order to succeed, it is important that you have a job that you can enjoy. If you are one of those people who hates your job, you have two courses of action. Either strive to change your reactions to the job, or *find another job*. If you don't, it will be very difficult for you to maintain a productive, upbeat attitude or to be fulfilled.

Remembering that attitude is the outward reflection of your internal thoughts and feelings, let's start with the working relationship that probably impacts you the most, that with your boss. If you enjoy your work and have a positive, pleasant demeanor, the chances are good your boss will notice. Employees who take on challenges without complaint, inspire others with their outlook, and treat people with respect will stand out. Employees who voluntarily arrive a little early or stay a little late to finish a project are noticed. Employees who work and don't count the minutes until the next break are recognized. Employees who respond positively to their boss's suggestions, requests, and criticisms make themselves invaluable.

Attributes like these can greatly enhance how you are perceived. In today's business world, with so many quality people to choose from, what often differentiates one employee from one another is attitude. *Sometimes attitude speaks louder than skill.*

In the blanks below, list specific ways you can show your positive attitude in the workplace. What concrete actions can you take to create a more pleasant work atmosphere and impress your supervisors?

SHORT-TERM ACTIONS   LONG-TERM ACTIONS

1._____   1._____

2._____   2._____

3._____   3._____

4._____   4._____

5._____   5._____

A negative attitude doesn't only radiate outward and affect others' perceptions of you, a negative attitude also permeates inward and affects how you work. If you tend to focus on problems and weaknesses at your work, then soon your negative attitude could affect your perception of *yourself*. If your outlook is constantly bleak, you'll eventually start to believe you're to blame. If you are sure that, despite your best efforts, something will always go wrong, then your self-esteem will begin to suffer. You'll feel helpless and defeated. You may not work as hard or you may try to overcompensate and make mistakes.

EXAMPLE - John was hired for his expertise in word processing. He was well-educated and very skilled at his job. His speed and efficiency made him one of the best in his office. In each of his first three years with the firm, John had received a modest Christmas bonus. However, this year he didn't get one. John began to falter. He felt he was passed over for the bonus because of a mistake he had made. In reality, in an attempt to cut its overhead, the firm had discontinued Christmas bonuses. But instead of inquiring about the bonus, John racked his brain trying to figure out what he might have done wrong. When he couldn't isolate the reason, he began to wonder if his efficiency had 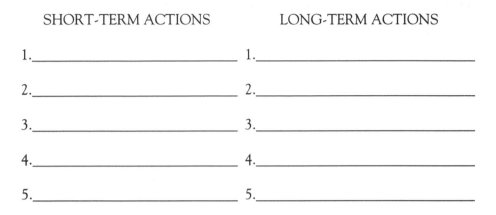 diminished. Soon, John dwelt on that thought every day and began making mistakes he'd never made before. This multiplied his feelings of inadequacy. Eventually his confidence and self-esteem suffered.

In this situation, John allowed an event that happened at work to dampen his normally confident attitude which, without good cause, turned into self-doubt, which then affected his on-the-job performance. A negative attitude can permeate inward and decrease your effectiveness at work.

Now let's explore another way attitude can affect your life. A negative state of mind can affect a person physically, by causing a loss of stamina. People with bad attitudes often make statements like: "I have to *work* much too *hard*." "I'm so *tired* of working on this job." "I'm *sick* of this project." "This report's going to be the *death of me*." The mind is a very powerful thing. It's been clinically proven time and time again that the mind can directly affect our health for the better or for the worse. If you tell yourself constantly that you're *tired* of this or *sick* of that, eventually you <u>will</u> physically become tired or sick. You'll begin to find your stamina is decreasing. *You are the most influential person in your life.* The key is to break out of the cycle. Tell yourself that you *have* energy and vitality. Tell yourself that you feel strong enough to handle any tasks you may face. Include words like endurance, power, energy, speed and strength in your inner monologue. Another solution is to approach the loss of stamina from a *physical* standpoint. In Chapter 8 you'll learn about the physical aspects of positive attitude.

EXTERNAL FACTORS THAT AFFECT ATTITUDE

Besides negative people, what other factors negatively affect your attitude? This can be a very difficult question to answer because attitude is ever-changing. *Attitude is not a static attribute; it is an on-going process.* Many times it's a challenge to pinpoint the specific factors that directly and perceptibly change your attitude. Sometimes there are several subtle factors that, when combined, may transform your attitude from a positive one to a negative one within the course of a day. Or, a single event could act as a catalyst that polarizes your outlook in an instant.

EXAMPLE - Sara arose one morning after a good night's sleep and got ready for work. She felt good physically and her attitude was decidedly positive. She was looking forward to the challenges that awaited her at work. When she arrived at her office, she discovered an open window near her desk. Unfortunately there had been a rainstorm the night before and as a result, the wind had scattered the files that were on her desk all over the floor. Many of them were also wet. Even  though the files were still readable and there was no permanent damage, Sara became extremely angry. It impacted her attitude for the rest of the day.

Everyone experiences frustrating moments like these that trigger a rush of negative thoughts and feelings. For Sara, the sight of her scattered files triggered an instantaneous negative reaction — one that may or may not have been justified. Regardless, the incident consumed her thoughts and feelings for the rest of the day.

In the space provided below, write down instances when you allowed your negative attitude to impact everything you did for a day or more.

Next, place an "O" by the instances where you overreacted, an arrow "➡" when your reactions negatively impacted someone else, and an asterisk "*" by those items that you have since handled more positively. Then make notes of what you wish to do the next time those situations arise.

INCIDENT	AFFECT	NEXT TIME...
1._____	_____	_____
2._____	_____	_____
3._____	_____	_____
4._____	_____	_____
5._____	_____	_____
6._____	_____	_____
7._____	_____	_____
8._____	_____	_____
9._____	_____	_____
10._____	_____	_____

- THE CHAPTER IN BRIEF -

* Discover how others' attitudes affect you.
* "Remember, no one can make you feel inferior without your consent." You alone control your attitude.
* Attitude definitely affects one's level of success in personal relationships.
* Sometimes attitude speaks louder than skills.
* Attitude can affect a person's job performance and level of success.
* A negative attitude can undermine confidence and lead to self-doubt.
* <u>You</u> are the most influential person in your life.

TWO

HOW TO CONTROL YOUR ATTITUDE

ACCENTUATE THE POSITIVE...

3

As we mentioned earlier, you are the most influential person in your life and you are capable of changing your attitude. Knowing that, who wouldn't want to make the effort to have a positive attitude? Who wouldn't want to be perceived as pleasant, successful, friendly, and a winner? All you need are some solid strategies on how to alter and control your attitude.

The first step to building a positive attitude comes from the old philosophy, "*Accentuate the positive and eliminate the negative.*" Wiser words were never spoken. There are always going to be positive *and* negative events that confront you every day. There will always be problems in life that you will be forced to concentrate on and deal with. The key is to learn the difference between concentrating on a problem and dwelling on it. To concentrate on a problem is to focus your energy on solving it and getting on with your life. To dwell on a problem means you become consumed with what went wrong and how distressing the situation has become. A negative person will focus on the past and want to analyze how the problem occurred, pointing out every miserable detail and complaining about its effects.

To create a positive frame of mind, you must accept what has happened, forget about the past, and look to the future. We can all learn from our experiences. It's important to set your mind and energy to solving problems and preventing them from happening again. But avoid the trap of dwelling on problems from the past. Reliving experiences from the past only gives them a firmer foothold in your subconscious mind.

In *The Self-Talk Solution* Shad Helmstetter states, "The human brain does not know the difference between a real experience and an experience that is created or *re-created* in the mind." So as each problem arises, write down a specific strategy for solving it and set priorities for each course of action. Once the problem has been solved, create a strategy to prevent its happening again. Then, *forget about it.* As you work, consciously search for the positive side of the situation and downplay its discouraging side. This type of thinking will ignite your enthusiasm. It is good training for taking on new challenges with a fresh and vital approach.

Here's a strategy to help you focus positively at the start of each day. Arrive at work ten minutes early every morning. Sit at your desk or workspace quietly and mentally prepare for the day. Look over your schedule and responsibilities and focus on the positive points you'll encounter throughout the day. Consciously attempt to eliminate any negative thoughts or worries. As co-workers begin to arrive, greet each of them with a smile. Others will begin to seek you out each morning if they know you will greet them with a pleasant attitude and a smile.

Be careful not to fall into the trap of focusing on events beyond your work day. In the morning don't start focusing on a party you're going to attend that evening. It will just make your entire day a prelude to the party. You'll never fully focus on your job. In fact, you may find yourself rushing through your work or just hoping the day would hurry up and end. This is not a positive strategy, because it turns your job into an obstacle to your happiness.

Since even the most positive morning attitude can deteriorate by late afternoon, *it is important for you to make several "attitude checks" throughout the day.* An attitude check is simply taking a moment to ask yourself how you feel. What is your current state of mind and how is that reflected in your attitude? Often your attitude may have changed without your knowledge. You may not realize that you are suddenly clenching your teeth or curling your toes in your shoes.

Complete an attitude check by writing short answers to the questions below.

ATTITUDE CHECK

1. What word would I use to describe my emotions right now?
   Happy? Sad? Angry? Depressed? Bored?_____

2. Am I anticipating some important event in the near future?
   _____

3. If so, how do I feel about that event?_____

4. Is there any tension in my body right now?_____

5. What's the most positive thing that has happened to me
   today?_____

6. What's the most negative thing that has happened to me
   today?_____

7. Which event has affected me more, the positive or the
   negative?_____

After each Attitude Check, you must decide if you need to alter your current mind set. If you discover that you have a bad attitude you should immediately seek out a way to help change it to a positive one. There are many ways to do that. It may be as simple as taking several deep breaths and refocusing on the positive things that might happen the rest of the day. You can take a short walk, call a friend, or practice a relaxation technique.

If none of these suggestions work, *try finding "positive mental triggers."* A positive mental trigger is any person, place, or event from your life that evokes strong, positive, mental images or emotions. Many psychologists call it "Your Happy Place." It is a memory or clear image that you recall at will, focus on exclusively, and it helps you relax and brings a smile to your face. A positive mental trigger can quickly transform a negative attitude into a positive one. This is not an easy technique; it definitely takes practice. Your positive mental trigger should be very specific and intensely personal. You can't just think of "the fun you had last summer" or "that wonderful vacation in Florida." You need to be much more specific.

POSITIVE MENTAL TRIGGERS

Take the time to recall, create, or construct a list of possible positive mental triggers for yourself. Come up with intense, specific images that immediately bring a smile of joy to your face. Carefully construct every tiny detail in your image. Use all of your senses. If your positive mental trigger is your vacation in Florida: What exact day was it? What time was it? Where was the sun? How did the sand feel beneath your feet? How did the ocean smell? Was the wind blowing?

MY POSITIVE MENTAL TRIGGERS

1. _____

_____

_____

2. _____

_____

_____

3. _____

_____

_____

Now that you have specific positive mental triggers for yourself, practice using them. Find time to rehearse bringing those images to the forefront of your mind in vivid and pleasing detail. You never know when employing a positive mental trigger could turn your whole day around.

Another way to overcome negative thinking is simply to build up confidence

in yourself. Make a list below of your best attributes and qualities. Also list unique skills or talents you have that set you apart from others.

CONFIDENCE BUILDING LIST

My qualities are...	My skills are...	My talents are...
_____	_____	_____
_____	_____	_____
_____	_____	_____
_____	_____	_____
_____	_____	_____
_____	_____	_____
_____	_____	_____
_____	_____	_____
_____	_____	_____

Make a copy of your confidence building list and put it in your purse or wallet. Always carry it with you. Look at that list at least once a day to reassure yourself and build up confidence.

Believe in yourself and what you can do! Take pride in who you are. Use positive self-affirmation and kick the habit of putting yourself down. Unfortunately we often live and work in environments where there are plenty of people who are more than willing to put us down. Don't perpetuate that ugliness! Don't help others tear down your confidence! First, when someone insults you, let it roll off your back. Don't let it make you angry. Second, politely inform the person that you didn't appreciate the comment. Finally, reaffirm yourself by looking at your confidence building list.

You are your own best friend, so treat yourself that way. Don't become your own worst enemy by getting into the habit of self-criticism. Norman Vincent Peale calls it, "The Power of Positive Thinking." The Reverend Jesse Jackson expressed it by popularizing the simple but powerful phrase, "I am somebody!" Whatever you want to call it, however you express it, *you must believe in yourself.* You must believe that you are a special and unique individual with a combination of thoughts, skills and talents that no one else in the world has. Only *you* can truly validate your own life. Remind yourself daily that you're successful. You'll succeed. Tell yourself daily that you are a winner, and you'll win. Good, old fashioned self-confidence is one of the easiest ways to capture and maintain a positive attitude. Try it!

- THE CHAPTER IN BRIEF -

*Accentuate the positive.
*Start each day by focusing on the positives of your job.
*Make several attitude checks daily.
*Find a positive mental trigger.
*Believe in yourself.

...ELIMINATE THE NEGATIVE

4

A person who constantly dwells on the negative aspects of life will often find himself worrying a lot. A person whose bad attitude causes her to focus on all of her problems will have trouble finding much joy in life. Neither of these people will be happy with the results of projects at work or at home. They *will* be prime candidates for stress.

It's important to realize that stress is not confined to the realm of high-powered business or disastrous situations. Stress can affect anyone with a negative outlook on life; anyone who can't find relief from tension and channel energies in a positive, productive way.

What exactly is stress? How does it affect us physically? By definition, stress is simply an urgency, emphasis, or intense effort that induces bodily or mental reaction. Psychologists have linked stress directly to an innate, human "fight-or-flight response." Herbert Benson, M.D., director of the Hypertension and Behavioral Medicine Sections at Boston's Beth Israel Hospital, describes that innate fight-or-flight response as a "physiological reaction to danger which raises blood pressure, heart rate, and breathing, speeds blood flow to muscles, and prepares the body to fight or run. Useful to early humans against physical threats in the environment, it is less necessary in the modern world where stresses are largely mental."

This natural response also can be found in the animal kingdom. When a cat arches its back and hisses at potential danger, it is displaying that basic fight-or-flight form of stress. However, in most cases when animals experience stress, they use it, release it, and get on with their lives.

Unfortunately, modern day human beings don't have the latitude to respond as naturally as animals do. However, the stress release pattern animals have can be used as a goal or model in our everyday life.

EXAMPLE - Bob has just arrived at work after a restless and sleepless night. On his desk he finds a memo from his boss telling him that the report he'd worked on for a week and a half was "insufficient and poorly organized." The memo concludes by saying that he has two days to rewrite it entirely.

Bob's attitude deteriorates and he begins to experience some stress. Just then, the door opens and his boss enters. Fuming, the boss verbally reprimands Bob for his consistently unsatisfactory work. Bob's stress increases rapidly. His heart-rate speeds up and his breathing becomes more shallow and labored. At this point, if Bob were living in a prehistoric society and were allowed to react instinctively, he might leap up onto his desk and growl ferociously while tearing the report — or perhaps even his boss — apart with his teeth. Unfortunately in today's more civilized world, this is an inappropriate and unacceptable response to stress!

Bob, like most of us, will restrain his fight-or-flight response and internalize the stress instead. It is this repression of a natural physical reaction which, over the course of time, causes some of the classic symptoms of stress mismanagement: damage to the circulatory system, the digestive tract, the lungs, the muscles, and the joints. For instance, chronic stress can directly affect your heart and lead to coronary artery disease. Robert Eliot, M.D., director of the cardiovascular unit of the Swedish Medical Center in Denver, Colorado, says that, "The stress reaction actually takes bites out of the heart muscles. It can overcontract the small muscle fibers until some of them rip." Stress also adversely affects the digestive system. People who worry and react negatively are more susceptible to the formation of ulcers. Charles T. Richardson, M.D., of the Dallas Veterans Administration Medical Center says, "In those who develop ulcers, emotional distress may lead to a breakdown in the way the stomach and duodenum protect themselves against acid secretion. In other words, stress—or specifically, the physiological reaction to stressful events—may interfere with the defense mechanism in some way." Even the less intricate parts of your body suffer when you are unable to rid yourself of damaging stress. Your muscles tend to tighten up in particularly stressful situations. This in turn causes painful tension and for many people leads to back pain. "Over a period of time, a chronically tensed muscle may lose its stretch and become shortened," states Lawrence W. Friedmann, M.D., in *Freedom from Backaches*. This tension leads to a much higher risk of injury.

Stress affects everyone differently. Take the time now to consider exactly how stress affects you. Be specific and make a list of these things that cause stress in your life and how you react to them. But be cautious. Don't trust your feelings. Approach this task from an objective, intellectual point of view. You can't always trust your feelings when it comes to dealing with attitude and stress. Think back in your recent past to a time when you were experiencing great amounts of negative stress. Ask yourself if you were able to think calmly and rationally about that stress as you were feeling it. If you're like most people, in times of extreme stress, your emotions take over. The result is a distorted view of the situation. To ensure an accurate assessment, force yourself to be clinical and logical when making your list.

Next, you need to gather some data. Get input from others. Ask your spouse or a co-worker how they perceived your actions during a time of negative stress. If they respond in a strictly judgmental way, ask for more specific input. For instance, if you get an answer like, "That was an awful way to behave," you need to ask, "Yes, but what specifically did I do? How did I react? If you had to make a guess, what do you think caused my reaction?" By gathering data about yourself from others, you won't have to rely solely on your feelings.

Don't do this exercise if you still have a negative attitude. The responses you get may raise your stress level. Wait until you are calm and ready to discuss your actions objectively. Try to choose a time and place that is good for both you and the person from whom you're soliciting input.

Once you have an accurate assessment of how stressful situations negatively affect your life, seek active ways to eliminate those bursts of stress when they occur. Stress must be actively eliminated from the mind and body. One way to accomplish this is simply to *breath.* In stressful situations, breathing usually becomes labored and shallow. Some individuals even reach the point of hyperventilation when they are stressed. When you feel your stress level beginning to rise, stop and take control of your breathing. Sit down, inhale slowly through your nose on a count of seven. Let the air drop deep into your lower lung and stomach area. Then instead of actively exhaling, just let the air flow out through your mouth naturally. Repeat this exercise three or four times before you continue with your day.

In their book, *The Doctor's Guide to Instant Stress Relief*, the authors Ronald G. Nathan Ph.D, Thomas E. Staats, Ph.D., and Paul J. Rosch, M.D., suggest *buying or making a relaxation tape to listen to during those times when you are experiencing general or prolonged periods of stress.* "It is fun to add not only instrumental music but also environmental sounds. Try taping waves lapping against the shore, crickets chirping in the night, or rain dancing on a metal roof...whatever you find most relaxing." Another way to dissipate stress immediately is to *employ your positive mental trigger* that you created in Chapter 3. In Chapter 8 we'll discuss how *exercise* can eliminate the damaging effects of long-term stress.

SEPARATING WORK AND HOME LIFE

The next step to improving your attitude is to learn to eliminate residual occupational and domestic tension. That means the inability to separate work-related tensions from home-related tensions and vise versa. If you take work home with you and home to work with you, the only thing you'll accomplish is to make yourself ineffective in both places. Millions of Americans suffer from this problem. It's not unusual to find yourself thinking about an important work project while eating dinner at home. But doing that will affect your health and family relationships. It's quite common to allow an argument with a spouse or loved one to affect your mood at work. You'll find yourself unable to concentrate on your work because your mind and heart are at home. These habits are common, but also quite dangerous to maintaining a positive attitude.

John M. Rhoads, professor of psychiatry at Duke University School of Medicine, conducted a study regarding the ability to control attitude and stress. He chose a group of fifteen men he knew personally to be "effective, successful, and physically and mentally healthy." The group consisted of corporate vice-presidents, physicians, lawyers, and professors. Each man worked at least sixty hours a week. Next, he chose a second group of fifteen men who worked equally long hours but who were displaying signs of overwork, fatigue, bad attitude, and unusual amounts of negative stress. Rhoads had each group complete an in-depth questionnaire on lifestyle, attitude toward work, and personality. The results revealed that long hours of work are not what make people ill. It's the way people are able to *control their attitude and stress.* According to Rhoads, "Perhaps the most striking of these personality features, is the ability to *postpone thinking about problems until it is appropriate to deal with them.* All the healthy, successful subjects had this ability. In contrast, the overworked men were never free of ruminating or of being obsessed about work problems, often to the point that it interfered with the ability to do anything else."

Learn how to separate your work from your home life. Learn how to turn your stress on and off. Let go of your stress and move on to other things when it's appropriate to do so. The ultimate goal is to have the control similar to that of a water faucet.

What are some specific ways to master this ability of "separation"? One way is to build transitional times into your day. It was suggested earlier that you schedule a ten-minute slot each morning to prepare for the workday. This is very helpful for individuals who have trouble separating work from home. You should also build-in a transitional time slot at the end of the workday before you go home. If you've had a particularly rough workday, spend at least ten minutes to make the transition between work and home. Use this time to readjust your attitude. Play relaxing music on your car radio, listen to a relaxation tape, breath, or focus on your positive mental trigger. If you're still tense once you get home, take time there to adjust to your day. If you have children or someone else who is demanding your time, explain that you need ten minutes of quiet time after which you will be happy to be with them.

Another way to separate work and home is to make a list of your home or work-related problems before going to one place or the other. For instance, if you have several unpleasant things you know you have to deal with at work in the near future, write them down on a piece of paper at the end of the day. Also write down any possible solutions you can think of at the moment. Then take the piece of paper, fold it up, and put it in your desk. Release yourself from those responsibilities before you go home. The note will remind you of the actions you need to take tomorrow. Try to solve home-related problems after work hours as much as possible. This also will keep home separate from your workday. Some-times using physical symbolism can help you adjust your attitude. At the very least, you should always make a thorough attitude check before going from work to home or vice versa.

PURGING PET PEEVES

What really makes you angry? What are the triggers that set you off immedi-ately with little thought? What are those little things in your life that evoke instant, almost irrational rage? In other words, what are your worst...PET PEEVES?!

We all have pet peeves, though a pet peeve for one person may have little or no affect on another person. We don't want pet peeves. We don't seek them out. But somehow they sneak into our lives and pop up causing frustration and anger.

EXAMPLE - Jerry is just finishing his morning coffee and toast. The sun is shining, the birds are chirping, the coffee is hot, and the toast isn't burnt. Life is good. When he finishes, he proceeds to the bathroom to brush his teeth. He's whistling cheerfully. He opens the medicine cabinet. Then suddenly, he sees it: THE TOOTHPASTE TUBE SQUEEZED FROM THE MIDDLE! He bounds down the stairs to punish the culprit, his wife, but finds she has already left for work. Jerry's day has been devastated.

EXAMPLE - Betty comes home from work for lunch. She eats at the kitchen table then ascends the stairs to brush her teeth. She squeezes the tube from the middle and brushes, while humming cheerfully. Suddenly she notices it: THE BATH TOWEL LYING IN THE MIDDLE OF THE BATHROOM FLOOR! She stomps down the stairs angrily muttering about her husband's annoying habit and goes back to work. Betty's afternoon has been devastated.

Jerry and Betty each have a pet peeve that the other always seems to forget. Each has a strong, instantaneous reaction to their particular pet peeve that causes a complete attitudinal swing. This, you would say, is irrational behavior. Squeezing the toothpaste tube from the middle hurts nothing. It doesn't diminish the effectiveness of the toothpaste or the tube itself. It's a "little inconvenience" at best. The same is true of the towel. On a *bad* day it might be considered "slightly bothersome." Jerry and Betty are no different from you or your spouse, significant other, friend, etc. Pet peeves have amazing power to change attitude. To prove it, write your pet peeves in the blanks and then give each a rank between 1 and 5: 1 being mildly annoyed to 5 being extremely upset. BE HONEST.

MY PERSONAL PET PEEVES

PET PEEVE   RANKING

1._____   _____

2._____   _____

3._____   _____

4._____   _____

5._____   _____

Now go back through your list (STILL BEING BRUTALLY HONEST), and circle those pet peeves which are completely based in rational thought. Circle the pet peeves which you can completely and without reservation, reasonably justify as normal reactions. Then circle the pet peeves that are rooted in well-conceived logic. If you're like most people, there are no pet peeves that are circled right now.

Recognizing that almost all pet peeves are illogical and irrational, knowing that our normal reactions to them serve no justifiable cause, and understanding that they instantly damage our attitude, why do we continue to allow them to exist? It comes down to a matter of will. You must eliminate those irrational feelings that are a constant assault on your attitude. *Dissect each pet peeve, look at it closely in the grand scheme of things, and then formulate a plan to eliminate your reaction to it.* Look back over you pet peeve list and write your elimination plans next to each pet peeve in the blanks below.

PET PEEVE   PLAN TO ELIMINATE YOUR REACTION

1._____   _____

2._____   _____

3._____   _____

4._____   _____

5._____   _____

Remember, you won't be able to eliminate your pet peeves in one day. Some habits die hard and it's easy to cling to pet peeves as if they were gold coins. But if and when you can relieve yourself of the anger and frustration they bring, you will surely have a much more positive outlook and a happier life.

- THE CHAPTER IN BRIEF -

* Discover how stress affects you.
* Use transitional times, attitude checks, relaxation
  techniques and tapes, proper breathing and positive
  mental triggers to eliminate stress.
* Completely separate work life from home life.
* Postpone thinking about problems until the time is right to deal with
  them.
* Eliminate pet peeves and the attitude problems they inject into
  your life.

BE PREPARED, PLAN AHEAD

5

Have you ever walked into a meeting or interview unprepared? How many times have you been given an assignment or project to work on and missed your deadline? When was the last time you had to make a presentation or pitch an idea and wished you had more time to plan? How did each of the previous situations make you feel? It was probably extremely difficult to maintain a positive attitude. Everyone knows the stress of being unprepared. Everyone knows the advantage of planning ahead. Yet how often do you find yourself in situations like the ones above? It takes a great deal of will power to make sure you are prepared for every project or problem you will face each day. Of course there will be surprises in life that not even the most organized person can be prepared for. But those who do take the time and effort to plan ahead, find that a positive mental attitude is a natural by-product of being prepared.

Make a list of the major upcoming projects or tasks that you face this week. Beside each project, write down at least three specific ways you can prepare to accomplish it. Next write down any perceived road blocks in the way of achieving your goal. Then write solutions to those road blocks. This could include anything from time constraints to uncooperative co-workers, to inadequate instructions, to your own negative attitude.

PROJECT   ROAD BLOCKS   SOLUTIONS

1._____   _____   _____

                  _____   _____

                  _____   _____

2._____   _____   _____

                  _____   _____

                  _____   _____

3._____   _____   _____

                  _____   _____

                  _____   _____

There is no mystery or magic to this process. It's simply a matter of *being strict with yourself, preparing and planning ahead as much as possible.*

In this book you have been asked to make several lists. The decision to have you do that is not a random choice. It is by design. *Lists are excellent tools to help you visualize and articulate your thoughts and feelings.* Our minds are incredible machines. The speed with which our brain can process information is mind-boggling! This is a good thing, since literally millions of bits of information pass through your mind in a single day. And so, although many excellent ideas, concepts, and strategies are certain to occur to you, you would be hard pressed to remember them all. That's where lists can assist you. The items you write down on a list are there for the duration. You can refer back to them and respond to them at your own pace. Never underestimate the value of making lists for yourself.

THE PITFALLS OF PROCRASTINATION

Simply making a list of how to prepare is only half the battle. You must *act* on it. The biggest obstacle to the best laid plans is PROCRASTINATION! Why do we procrastinate? Because we underestimate the time required to complete a task, dread a certain task, or fear it.

EXAMPLE - Cindy was an efficient, conscientious worker. She had a great attitude about her job and always seemed prepared. Her secret, of course, was planning ahead. One Wednesday morning her boss gave her a large project to complete by Friday afternoon. Cindy immediately canceled the appointment she had on Friday morning and blocked out the entire day to work on the project. She even set aside some planning time on Thursday. She had time on Wednesday to complete the project but chose to wait. Unfortunately for Cindy, when she arrived at work on Friday prepared to work on the project, she found that her computer was down. Now she would be forced to do the project on an old typewriter which would take twice as long and look half as professional. In addition, there were files in the computer that she needed to access. Needless to say, Cindy was unable to complete the project on time and risked the anger of her boss.

Most people have had similar experiences. Cindy did everything right except one thing; she procrastinated. As it turned out, that procrastination caused her a lot of grief and easily affected her attitude and the attitude of her boss. Once again, there is no magical formula that needs to be employed here just a simple message, *"Don't procrastinate!"*

In *Being the Best*, Denis Waitley lists several ways to break out of the "procrastination rut": 1. Set your wake-up time a half hour earlier tomorrow, and leave it at the earlier setting. Use this time to think about the best way to spend your day. 2. Memorize and repeat this motto: Action TNT—Action Today, Not Tomorrow. 3. Concentrate all your energy and intensity, without distraction, on the successful completion of your current major project. Finish what you start. 4. Seek out and talk, in person, to a successful role model and mentor. The most productive people are those who learn from the successes and setbacks of others. 5. Understand that FEAR is False Education Appearing Real and that LUCK is Laboring Under Correct Knowledge. The more information you have on any subject, especially successful case histories, the less likely you are to post-pone your decisions. 6. View problems as normal indications of change in progress.

Since society and business are changing rapidly, it's up to the individual to view change as normal and to see many of the changes taking place as positive rather than negative.

MANAGING YOUR TIME

Another way to help maintain a positive attitude is to *be an efficient manager of your time*. When you don't have enough time to accomplish what you want in life, it affects your whole outlook. It's very easy when you're running late for an appointment or feeling pressed for time to allow a negative attitude to sneak in. So, effective time management is a *must* for you to be successful at work and at home.

31

First of all, when you plan your day you should *always schedule in some emergency time slots*. Insert an empty ten-minute block of time here and there just in case something goes wrong or runs overtime. If you are one of those people who schedules everything back-to-back and down to the minute, you're asking for trouble. It's a fact of life that surprises and unexpected problems will arise. And while it may be true you can't prepare for unexpected problems, *you can prepare for the extra time it may take to solve them*. You do that by scheduling in some empty time slots throughout your day.

Now you might be asking, "What if no problems arise? Won't I have wasted my time by allowing unscheduled time slots during my day?" Not at all!! If everything goes well and no problems occur, you can *use* that empty ten-minute time slot to prepare for your next appointment or project. Or you can use the time to do an Attitude Check and activate your Positive Mental Trigger. You can use the extra time to do anything productive! Wouldn't you welcome a quiet ten minutes in the midst of a stressful day? So schedule in some downtime for yourself; you'll be glad you did.

EFFECTIVE SCHEDULING

Using the space below, carefully schedule your next workday, including your time at home in the morning and evening. Make sure to schedule in strategic emergency time slots, Attitude Checks, and Positive Mental Triggers. Also write down how best to utilize your emergency time slots if no emergencies arise.

A.M.

12:00_____

1:00_____

2:00_____

3:00_____

4:00_____

5:00_____

6:00_____

7:00_____

8:00_____

9:00_____

10:00_____

11:00_____

P.M.

Noon_____

1:00_____

2:00_____

3:00_____

4:00_____

5:00_____

6:00_____

7:00_____

8:00_____

9:00_____

10:00_____

11:00_____

An integral part of effective time management is the use of *checklists and planners*. Both are invaluable tools for improving your outlook on life. Checklists let you keep track of exactly what needs to be done. If your work involves managing many projects at *once*, you'll find that a checklist not only allows you to plan effectively, but also makes it easy to set *priorities*. When you make your checklists, number your tasks in order of priority. Otherwise, how will you know which to tackle first? Try to use clean notebook-size paper for your checklists. Don't scribble them down on a napkin, a small piece of paper, or the back of another list. You are inviting disaster if your checklist isn't clear, in priority order, and easy to keep track of.

Consider shopping around to find a pocket planner, organizer, a desk calendar — anything that helps you organize the activities in your life. All of these things can help you visualize your tasks and make it much easier to set priorities. There's no better feeling than having your daily schedule, your project checklists, and other pertinent information at your fingertips at all times. Being confident in how your time is planned results in a positive attitude.

It's extremely important how you set your mind as you plan and prepare for each day. A general rule of thumb is to *"expect the best, but be prepared for the worst."* In other words, think positively, but realistically. Unrealistic optimism is just as bad *or worse* than defeatist pessimism. Extreme optimists who think absolutely everything will succeed are in for a long, hard road of bitter disappointments; and the total pessimist who "knows" that everything will go wrong, leaves little possibility for complete success.

Neither optimism nor pessimism alone will get you through life successfully. You must balance the two.

- THE CHAPTER IN BRIEF -

* Be prepared and plan ahead.
* Don't procrastinate.
* Be an efficient manager of your time.
* Schedule emergency time slots throughout the day.
* Use checklists and planners to improve your level of confidence.
* Learn to set priorities for projects.
* Expect the best, but be prepared for the worst.

SET REALISTIC GOALS

6

I n the introduction to this book, we stressed the importance of goal-setting when you wish to make changes in your life. Remember the last time you achieved a major goal in your life? Do you remember how good that felt? How wonderful it was to have your hard work pay off? You probably had a positive attitude for days. And it was something you didn't have to consciously think about or work at. Wouldn't it be great if you could capture that feeling every day. You can...well, maybe not with the same level of intensity, but it is possible to obtain that kind of positive attitude and feeling of accomplishment every day. You can achieve this by setting daily realistic goals for yourself.

Psychologists say we should have a number of major, long-range goals to have a healthy, fulfilling life. In addition, we need some medium- range goals with specific dates in mind for achieving them. But, while most people have thought about their long-range goals: to own a house, to own a nice car, to achieve job security, to raise a family, etc., few of us have set specific medium-range goals. Nor do we set daily or short- term goals for ourselves. The advantage of setting a lot of realistic, short-term goals is that we feel we constantly are *succeeding.* Daily, achievable goals help build positive attitude. Good goal-setting and achievement give forward momentum to our lives.

Take a look at your long-range goals and big projects. With these larger, tougher goals you need to *use the "divide and conquer" technique.* Are you feeling overwhelmed by the goal of building a new house or boosting sales by 50 percent? Who wouldn't be intimidated by tall orders like these? As magnificent as our minds are, they can't always visualize and grasp huge goals. The key is to divide each project into its smallest common denominators and translate them into realistic, short-term goals. For instance, with the house-building project you might begin with the short-term goal of scouting out suitable locations. Your next goal might be to make appointments with prospective contractors. These are realistic goals that you have a much better chance of achieving.

GOAL-SETTING

Take one of your major projects or long-range goals and divide it into three medium-range goals. Then subdivide each of these into easily attainable short-range goals. Now set specific dates for achieving all of the goals. You'll be surprised at how smoothly you move toward achieving the ultimate goal. And the important thing is that you'll have a positive attitude about it throughout the process.

Long-Range Goal

_____

Medium-Range Goals

1._____   2._____   3._____

Short-Range Goals

a._____   a._____   a._____

b._____   b._____   b._____

c._____   c._____   c._____

After you set your goals and begin meeting them, the fun part begins. The most important part of the goal-setting process is the REWARD! *You must reward yourself on a daily basis each time you achieve one of your goals.* That's not  to say you take a cruise to the Bahamas every time you finish a report before the deadline. Measure the reward by the difficulty of each goal that is achieved.

For years psychologists have known the incredible power of positive reinforcement. Everyone is familiar with the story of how Pavlov proved the effectiveness of positive reinforcement with his famous dogs. Many of you already use the basic principles of this concept with your children and pets. You know the value of giving frequent and immediate rewards. But many people seem to overlook themselves. They work and slave at a job for a solid year, looking only to the reward of a two-week vacation. They fail to use the valuable positive-reinforcement techniques that they freely give to others. You need to reward yourself daily. Plan small, frequent rewards throughout the day. If you successfully complete a difficult task at work, take yourself out to dinner or a movie. Go out and have fun once in a while. Allow yourself some personal pleasures to help break up the monotony and build up your attitude. Herbert M. Greenburg, Ph.D., founder of Stress Management, in Carlsbad, California, calls these things pleasurable "goodies." For instance: music (listening to it, singing, or playing an instrument), laughter, poetry, sayings, and slogans (reading them), prayer (and other religious comfort), hugging (and other forms of touch), spending money (if you enjoy doing it), playing (with or without toys), hot baths and hot tubs (soaking in one), rest (sleep, catnaps, doing nothing), rituals and traditions (family, religious, or social ones).

If you don't give yourself some goodies, if you can't allow yourself to have some fun, all of your hard work will be in vain. And it will be very difficult to have a positive attitude about anything. So show yourself the same courtesy you probably give to others — reward yourself when you achieve a goal.

- THE CHAPTER IN BRIEF -

* Set realistic, short-range goals.
* Use the divide and conquer technique on huge projects and long-range goals.
* Reward yourself on a daily basis each time you achieve a goal.
* HAVE SOME FUN NOW AND THEN!

COMMUNICATE CLEARLY

7

A major influence on your daily attitude is your ability to communicate with co-workers and friends. Let's look at the more basic forms of communication and how they directly affect your attitude.

HOW MISCOMMUNICATION AFFECTS ATTITUDE

You know how frustrating it is to be misunderstood. You know how angry people sometimes can get over simple miscommunication. Your ability to express yourself is directly linked to your attitude. If you know how to make yourself understood and get what you want, then the chances of maintaining a positive attitude are high. But successful communication takes a great deal of concentration and a knowledge of the right skills.

THE MAJOR COMPONENTS OF COMMUNICATION

In order for you to make contact with the mind of another person you have four major tools: speaking, writing, listening, and reading. Each is a skill that must be learned. But only two — reading and writing — are taught in school. We receive little instruction for the general art of speaking. And what about listening? The art of listening is seldom taught in any educational institution. It's incredible how most of us assume that listening is a natural gift for which no training is required. We're going to concentrate here on these two untaught skills.

There are six basic components of spoken communication: *the source, the receiver, the message, the channel, feedback, and noise.* The source is you. The receiver is anyone with whom you are trying to communicate. The similarities or differences between the source and the receiver will directly affect their ability to communicate. When you must communicate with someone who is very different from yourself, what is your attitude? How do you approach those situations? Do you allow preconceived notions to influence your attitude? Since communication is a two-way process, the source and the receiver must overcome influencing attitudes to be successful.

Always discover the differences between you and your listener and strive to minimize them in conversation. This will improve the attitudes of both communicators.

The third component is the message or simply what you are trying to communicate. Words are the building blocks for messages. Words are not the *only* way to convey messages, but they carry the most weight. Shad Helmstetter underscores the importance of words in his book *The Self-Talk Solution:* "...every word you and I will ever hear, think, write, or speak will have a picture and a meaning attached to it which inform and stimulate...our subconscious minds. We are affected by our words—each and every one of them." Recognizing this fact, the words you use to communicate directly affect the attitude of the person you're speaking to. Choose your words carefully. Think before you speak. A careless or misplaced phrase could quickly change the mood of your listener and jeopardize the communication process.

The channel is "how" a receiver *receives* a message. It's important to know that *hearing is not the only channel through which your receiver gets your message.* All of the senses are involved. Your eyes see a speaker even though you receive most of the message through your ears. You may even smell the speaker. We can even receive strong messages using only sense memory. For instance, "long fingernails scraping down a chalkboard," or "rotten eggs" are two images that probably evoke strong sense memories for most people. Sense memories can greatly enhance or endanger effective communication. Using descriptive sense memory phrases allows you to make a very strong connection with your listener, providing he or she can relate to the images. The reverse can be true. If you unwittingly use sense memories which carry negative connotations for the listener, your rapport with that person could be greatly reduced. To communicate what you want, you need to be aware of exactly what your message is and through what channels it will be received.

Feedback gives us cues as to how things are going. *Feedback is critical to communication.* There is no communication unless a receiver responds to a message. Giving positive feedback to a "source" is reassuring and helps to bolster a positive attitude. Learn to be an active listener. When you have the opportunity in conversation, try to restate what has been said to you in your own words. This cuts down on miscommunication and assures the speaker that you are both listening and interested.

Feedback can be observed or imagined. It's important to know the difference. Observed feedback is hearing a listener laugh at your joke or seeing your boss use your idea. Imagined feedback is thinking someone dislikes you because he doesn't laugh at your joke or imagining your boss doesn't appreciate you because she rejects your idea. We often let our imagination get the best of us. So be careful. *Don't let imagined feedback affect your attitude.*

Feedback also can be immediate or delayed. Try to encourage immediate feedback — whether positive or negative. Pavlov and his dogs helped us to understand that, psychologically, immediate feedback always produces the best results. Just remember to analyze feedback calmly and rationally before making any changes in your attitude or the way you communicate.

Anything that prevents a message from making it from the source to the receiver is "noise." For instance, if you have an accent, your listener may not always be able to understand you. Or you may accidentally choose words that offend your listener, in which case your message is lost. In addition, your listener's attitude toward you will be immediately altered. If you are in a situation where you feel there is too much noise for your message to be communicated clearly, try to eliminate the noise or suggest to your listener that you continue your discussion at another time or place. It is better to delay a conversation than to risk a misunderstanding.

Research has shown that we generally remember 85 percent to 90 percent of what we see and only 15 percent to 20 percent of what we hear. And so, how you communicate nonverbally is as important as how you communicate with your voice. Body language says as much about attitude as what is being said. It takes on even greater importance when you are listening. There are gestures and body postures that clearly convey unspoken messages. The following exercise illustrates this concept.

BODY LANGUAGE

Match each description of body language to the attitude or emotion which it conveys by drawing a line between the two.

DESCRIPTION	EMOTION
1. Arms crossed. Legs crossed. Eyes toward the ceiling.	NERVOUS
2. Hands in lap. Head cocked to one side. Yawning. No particular eye focus. Slumped down in chair.	ANGRY
3. Foot tapping on floor. Hands fidgeting. Rapid eye movement from place to place.	BORED
4. Sharp, fixed-eye focus. Teeth clenched. Breathing heavy. Lips pursed.	UNRECEPTIVE
5. Furrowed brow. Mouth hung slightly open. Scratching head.	CONFUSED

You shouldn't have had much trouble completing the exercise. Each set of physical cues has an assumed, unspoken message. *So make sure that what you say with your body coincides with what you say with your words.*

Finally, to help yourself communicate clearly, always establish eye contact with your listener. *Your eyes are one of the most effective tools you have for communication.* They are very expressive and usually tell you what a person's attitude is.

Making eye contact with someone during conversation indicates your interest in wanting to communicate. How many times have you tried to give an important message to someone whose eyes are wandering around the room? You feel as if you and your message are unimportant to the listener. If you are unable to make eye contact, you miss out on half of the communication process. Always try to make that connection before you begin to speak. Let the other person know that you *care* about what you're communicating. Good, clear communication with others is a vital key to your success and a healthy attitude.

- THE CHAPTER IN BRIEF -

* The ability to communicate with others is a major influence on your daily attitude.
* Learn the six components of communication: The more similar the *source* and *receiver* are, the better the communication of the *message* will be. All of the senses can be *channels* for receiving the message. Know the difference between observed and imagined *feedback*. Be aware of how *noise* affects your communication.
* You remember 85 percent to 90 percent of what you see and only 15 percent to 20 percent of what you hear.
* Make sure your body language coincides with your verbal message.
* Make eye contact to ensure the clearest communication.

THE PHYSICAL ASPECTS OF A POSITIVE ATTITUDE

ven though attitude is a mind-set, there are several physical steps you can take to improve your attitude. And you'll also get the added extra of improving your physical health while you're at it. For years clinical tests have proven that if you think you *look* good; you'll *feel* good. It's a fact that a good attitude is closely linked with a healthy self-image. How do you feel about your physical appearance?

In the space provided, draw a self-portrait. Don't be concerned with artistic value. Just draw an approximate representation of your physical appearance. Next, place arrows by the areas of your body you want and have the ability to improve. Below the picture, write down the changes each arrow represents. Then list specific plans of action to change the area indicated by each arrow.

Things I would like to change about my appearance:

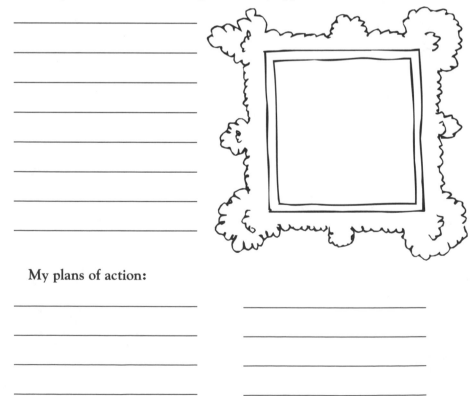

_____

_____

_____

_____

_____

_____

_____

My plans of action:

_____   _____

_____   _____

_____   _____

_____   _____

How do you think you appear to others? If you don't like your physical appearance, it's going to be very difficult to have a positive attitude. If there are areas of your physical appearance that really bother you, then alter them. You might be thinking you can't change your face or make yourself taller. You're right. There are many things about your physical appearance that you can't *change*. But there are a lot of things you can do to change the way you *feel* about yourself.

EXAMPLE - Jean was 27 pounds overweight. She had a big build with large bone structure. She tried and tried to lose weight but was never successful. Her doctor assured her that it wasn't her fault. He explained that some people's bodies and metabolisms prevent them from successfully losing weight. Jean's negative self-image grew until she fell into a depression. One day at the department store, a stranger who was standing next to her in line said, "Excuse me. I have to say this. I've been standing here noticing that you have the prettiest blue eyes I think I've ever seen." That was the trigger Jean needed. Suddenly her attitude began to change. A simple, positive statement from a stranger made her realize her weight was only one aspect of her physical appearance. With that thought, Jean began to wear blouses, hats, and scarves that accentuated and enhanced the beauty of her eyes. She also began to seek out clothing which made her look thinner. She even lost a couple of pounds with her new-found attitude. Jean is still overweight, but by accentuating the positive and minimizing the negative, she has a much better outlook on life.

Sometimes something as simple as a new hairstyle, a new suit, or a new pair of glasses can greatly affect your self-image. So if you aren't thrilled with your appearance, actively seek ways that will help you feel better about yourself. Experiment with your looks. Have fun. Take a bigger interest in the way you look; you'll feel much better for the effort.

Now draw a picture of the "ideal you." This is a portrait of what you <u>want</u> to look like.

THE "POSITIVE ATTRACTION" FACTOR

The most exciting part about this whole process is that when you *feel* better, you actually *look* better to others. When people have a healthy self-image and an enthusiastic, positive attitude, others will find them attractive. You must know someone who is not necessarily beautiful physically, but has a pleasant spirit about them. You are somehow drawn to them. People often describe them as attractive. We stated earlier that your attitude can speak louder than your skills. Well *your attitude can also speak louder than your physical appearance.* It's a wonderful cycle to be caught in. When you feel good about how you look, you'll look better to others, which will make you feel better about yourself, etc.

CHANNELING STRESS POSITIVELY

Throughout a normal workday, you will confront hundreds of different situations. Some will be expected, some surprises. Some will make you tense. Some will make you angry. Some will trigger your fight-or-flight response and cause you stress. When that happens, your body begins to release a potentially harmful substance known as noradrenaline. It is a hormone your brain releases into your body whenever you sense trouble. Redford B. Williams, M.D., professor of psychiatry at Duke University, states, "Everyday stressors can cause the release of this hormone. In lab experiments, we've found that noradrenaline can be released when people are given a difficult math problem to solve. This hormone is very easy to discharge, especially in today's society, where there are so many potential irritants."

The good news is that it's just as easy for your body to get rid of the hormone as it was to manufacture it. Dr. Williams continues, "Any physical expression that uses up calories, such as exercise, burns up the hormones instead of allowing them to get to the stage in the body where they can do harm. In this case, physical exercise is actually relaxing." *So the answer to burning up this toxic hormone, releasing stress, and improving your overall attitude is regular exercise.* A good exercise regimen allows you to blow off steam and helps you to relax when you're done.

Research has shown the types of exercise which are most conducive to blowing off steam are those that are both *aerobic and rhythmic.* Daniel M Landers, Ph.D., of the Exercise and Sports Research Institute, Department of Physical Education at Arizona State University, selected the thirty most popular forms of exercise. Of the thirty, he rated the following exercises the most beneficial for physical and mental health.

AEROBICS	ROPE SKIPPING
CALISTHENICS	ROWING
CIRCUIT TRAINING	RUNNING
CROSS-COUNTRY SKIING	SWIMMING
CYCLING	WALKING
HIKING WITH BACKPACK	

Choose an exercise that you enjoy doing. Don't exercise because you have to. Exercise because you want to. There are several techniques you can use to motivate yourself to want to exercise: 1. Refer to the self-portrait you drew at the beginning of this chapter. Remember *you* drew the portrait and listed what *you* felt needed to be improved. 2. Listen to your favorite music while you exercise. 3. Find a friend who will exercise with you. A friend will help motivate you and make the exercising experience more fun. 4. Set mini-goals for yourself. Don't expect to improve everything in a day. Know your limitations and set realistic exercise goals. 5. Make a list of the benefits you'll experience when you attain your goals. 6. Reward yourself when you reach your goals. You must have a positive attitude about exercising or you will defeat the whole purpose and minimize the benefits.

TIME TO RELAX

After you've worked hard and played hard, you need to be able to relax and replenish your body. *Having the ability to relax at any time is essential to maintaining a positive attitude.* Whenever you feel your stress rising and your attitude deteriorating, you should take a few moments and consciously relax yourself. Approach relaxation actively. Don't just slump down in a chair for a minute and take a few shallow breaths while thinking ahead about the rest of your day. Actively cause yourself to relax.

There are many different techniques you can master for taking a few moments to relax. One is to use your Positive Mental Trigger. Sit on that balmy beach or curl up in front of a roaring fire in a cozy cabin somewhere. Remember to be specific about details and mentally "be there" for a couple of minutes. Another method is to imagine a large dial in your mind. In times of peak stress, picture the dial on "High." Then over the course of a few relaxing moments, slowly turn your imaginary dial back down to "Low." Another relaxation method is to tense and release each muscle in your body. You can do this sitting at your desk: sit up straight in your chair, kick your shoes off, and place both feet flat on the floor. Then, beginning with your feet, and working your way up to your face, tense and relax your muscles. You may have your own private way to relax. Use any technique that helps you to relax and replenish your positive attitude.

One of the most important things you can do to help your attitude every day is to get a good night's sleep the night before. You know how tough it is to be upbeat and enthusiastic if you are tired and run down. Experts say we need a minimum of eight solid hours of sleep every night. If you are unable to get sufficient sleep, the consequences are obvious: physical and mental fatigue at work the next day, the inability to concentrate, and a negative attitude.

If you are like many people who work hard and experience stress, you may lie in bed for hours mulling over the problems of the day and worrying what may happen tomorrow. Learn to leave work-related problems outside the bedroom door. On particularly tough days, if you feel you absolutely must "unwind" mentally, then do it in a chair in another room. Peter G. Hansen, M.D., and well-known author recommends several aids in obtaining a good night's sleep:

1. Try to go to bed at the same time each night, preferably about half an hour before you plan to fall asleep.
2. Never use your bed as a desk. If you have paper work, do it at a desk or a table. Forcing yourself to stay alert while lying on your bed reinforces bad sleeping habits.
3. Have a warm drink (without alcohol or caffeine) at bedtime—hot milk is excellent. A relaxing warm bath can also help.
4. Leave your work problems at work; leave your home problems at the bedroom door.
5. Invest in a good quality, comfortable mattress. (Try all kinds, including waterbeds, before choosing one.) A mattress covering of real sheepskins can also upgrade the comfort of most beds. Comfortable pillows and quilts made of down can also help.
6. Keep your bedroom quiet in both noise levels and decoration.
7. Use your active relaxation techniques to slow your breathing and pulse rates.

Good physical habits will help you feel better about yourself. And a healthy self-image is at the root of a positive attitude.

- THE CHAPTER IN BRIEF -

* If you look good, you'll feel good.
* Attitude speaks louder than physical appearance.
* Exercise regularly to burn off toxic hormones, release stress and improve your attitude.
* Aerobic and rhythmic exercises are the best.
* Use active relaxation techniques.
* Get a good night's sleep, every night.

TAKE CONTROL AND CONQUER YOUR FEARS **9**

To have a positive attitude you must take control of your life and conquer your fears. When you feel you have control over your life, your attitude naturally improves. The basic concept of control is an interesting subject. Webster's *New Universal Dictionary* defines the verb control as follows: "To exercise authority over; direct; command." You can't be passive about success. You can't expect to be a winner if you sit quietly and wait for things to happen. Control is a wonderful tool if used correctly. When you have control of a situation it gives you confidence and alleviates the fear of the unexpected. But this theory also works in reverse. If you have confidence and think positively, you'll feel the power of control without actually doing anything to control the situation.

EXAMPLE- A psychological experiment was conducted recently to study the mental side of control. Two groups of workers were chosen to complete a series of mental tasks requiring a great deal of concentration. Both groups were exposed to loud, distracting background noise including machinery, traffic, and people speaking in foreign languages. One group had a button placed on their work desk so that they could turn off the background noise whenever they wanted to. The other group had no control button. The productivity of the group with the control button was considerably and consistently higher than the other group. This result, of course, was expected. But the most fascinating fact about this experiment is that none of the people **actually pushed the button**. Just *knowing* that the control button was there seemed to be enough!!

LEADING YOUR OWN LIFE

The lesson here is clear. Everyone needs some control buttons in their lives. When you feel out of control it's impossible to have a positive attitude about your life. Control buttons can be almost anything. *One of the best control buttons you have at your disposal is the word "No."* That small, two-letter word can become one of the most effective controlling tools in your arsenal. Linked directly with realistic goal-setting, the ability to say no helps you avoid overloading yourself and inviting failure. Saying no to an extra project at home or at work is not a sign of weakness. It doesn't mean that you don't care. It simply means that you are aware of your limitations at the present time and that accepting more work would place you well beyond them. When you know you're overloaded, say no. If you are in a work situation where you are unable to say no to your boss you should at least make him or her aware of your limits. When your boss gives you too many projects at one time, courteously say you will be unable to finish them all in time. Then ask your boss to tell you the priority for each individual project. This strategy will prevent you from being overwhelmed by the entire workload and allow you to begin with the

most important projects first. It's not easy learning how to say no. Just remember you should be kind and courteous, but also be firm.

Another control button you have is to *act, not react.* Don't allow life to *happen* to you. People with negative attitudes often consider themselves victims. Bad things always seem to happen to them. They don't really have any control over their lives, and so they are constantly reacting instead of acting. You need to learn to take hold of situations in your life and act upon them so they don't act on you. This is not something that will happen over night. You have to practice at taking control and accepting responsibility for your life. Yes, there will always be problems which arise. That's a part of living. But unless you become active in your life, you'll always encounter difficulties in heading off potential problems or being able to solve them once they arrive.

CONTROL

Make a list of the problems or negative situations you are currently facing. Think about each one carefully, then write down specific ways you can begin to take control of those events. What control buttons can you push to prevent those problems from arising again?

PROBLEMS   WAYS I CAN TAKE CONTROL

1._____   a._____
                               b._____
                               c._____

2._____   a._____
                               b._____
                               c._____

3._____   a._____
                               b._____
                               c._____

ELIMINATING "MOUNTAIN OUT OF MOLEHILL" THINKING

Another way to keep a sense of control in your life is: *don't sweat the little stuff.* That's a simplistic way of suggesting that you shouldn't focus your attention on trivial things and let their sheer number overwhelm you. Don't make mountains out of molehills. We mentioned earlier the importance of setting priorities in your life. Make sure you are spending your time and mental energy on those projects which are most important. Don't let all the little unimportant things that pester you sometimes get you down.

FEARS & PHOBIAS

We all have fears. They are a normal and natural part of life. Some of us are afraid of poisonous snakes. Some of us are afraid of guns. Others fear needles. These are all common, reasonable fears. However there is a great difference between a fear and a *phobia*. To be a happy, fulfilled person, you need to know the difference.

A phobia is an irrational dread of some thing or situation which wouldn't bother most people. Phobias include fear of heights, open or public spaces, the dark, dogs, cats, etc. If you have a phobia, you're not alone. The Phobia Society of America estimates there are thirteen million phobics. Now you may be thinking, "I'm not afraid of heights or public spaces or anything like that." But you might have a phobia and not know it. There are much more subtle, social phobias like the fear of public speaking, the fear of rejection, or the fear of failure.

Make a list below of the things that frighten you. Place a star by any fear you judge to be of the more irrational, phobic variety.

FEARS AND PHOBIAS

_____	_____
_____	_____
_____	_____
_____	_____
_____	_____

Those fears beside which you placed a star are the ones you must learn to confront and conquer. If you don't, you'll never have substantial control over your life. Robert DuPont, M.D., and author of the book _Phobias and Panic: A Physician's Guide to Modern Treatments_ explains that for most phobics "the worst fear is the _anticipation_ of what might happen." What he's talking about is the fear of fear. For instance, you may have a fear of rejection. You may be so afraid of what _might happen_ that you never ask anyone out on a date or never express your ideas to co-workers or boss. Once you've reached that extreme, you must confront and conquer your fear or it will begin to control you. Eventually you will even begin to avoid situations in which your fear might arise. And studies have shown conclusively that avoidance seldom works. Your phobias won't just disappear by avoiding them.

So, as in all other phases of your life you must act, not react. You must take control. In their book _Take Control of Your Life_ authors Sharon Faelten and David Diamond suggest three ways to deal with your phobias. First, try to _ride out the wave of anxiety_. Few phobics allow themselves to stay in their phobic situation long enough to realize their anxiety will go away in a minute or two. "So instead of saying, 'Oh my God, here it goes again,' and working yourself into a panic, say to yourself, 'As bad as I feel, this will pass.' And it will."

The second way of confronting a phobia is to _give yourself an "out."_ Jerilyn Ross, co-founder and president of the Phobia Society of America, says, "...most phobias are based on the fear of being in a situation where you believe you're trapped. And once trapped, you might have a panic attack. And during that attack you feel a loss of control, you fear embarrassing yourself, going crazy, or dying. But you can reduce that fear by arranging for a possible means of escape, _if_ you need one." For example, if you have a fear of public speaking and you know you'll be in a meeting where you'll be asked to share your ideas, prepare some crib notes for yourself or ask a colleague to be an audience _plant_ who will ask you all the right questions. Remember the experiment where two groups were asked to perform tasks with loud noises in the background? Remember how just _knowing_ they had a control button allowed one group to succeed? The same will work for you. You may not have to leave the situation, but knowing that you have an "out" will help to eliminate your fear.

Finally, don't drink alcohol to ease a fear or phobia. Dr. Ross points out that the more you drink, the more vulnerable you will feel, and the more likely you are to panic. Even one drink can slightly alter your judgment. "Also, caffeine triggers the release of adrenaline and has been linked to panic attacks." So avoid any source of caffeine before entering a phobic situation.

If all else fails, you should seek professional help. There is absolutely no shame in doing so. A final note to help alleviate any fears you have about your fears: In *Take Control of Your Life*, authors Faelten and Diamond say that with proper treatment, 90 percent of all phobics can achieve relief from their phobias.

- THE CHAPTER IN BRIEF -

* Aggressively take control of your attitude and your life.
* Learn how to say no.
* Act, don't react.
* Don't sweat the little stuff.
* Confront your fears and conquer them.
* Ride out the wave of anxiety.
* Give yourself an "out."
* Cut down on alcohol and caffeine.

HUMOR HELPS

10

Most experts agree that *a good sense of humor is essential to a healthy life.* A good burst of laughter brightens your countenance, lightens your attitude, and actually relieves stress. Research indicates that the simple act of *laughter increases the body's level of endorphins which ease the pain and improve the body's resistance to disease.* How about that! Who would have thought that something so simple and so fun could be so mentally and physically beneficial? But even if you aren't convinced of the scientific evidence, who can resist a silly giggle or a belly shaking guffaw now and then? We all need to laugh more often. It's pure joy and doesn't cost a dime.

Learn how to laugh, especially at yourself. Don't take yourself too seriously. Allow yourself to snicker when you make a stupid mistake. In the space provided on the following page, list some of your most embarrassing moments from your past that make you laugh today.

MOST EMBARRASSING MOMENTS

1. _____

   _____

2. _____

   _____

3. _____

   _____

By allowing yourself to laugh at an embarrassing moment you begin to realize that it isn't as horrible as you think. When faced with a trying situation people often say, "We'll look back and laugh at this someday." But the key is to laugh at those situations *when they happen*. Don't wait until later to find the humor in those instances. Think how much easier your life's embarrassing moments would have been had you been able to find the humor in the situation and laugh at yourself. You should be your own greatest source of humor.

Like other aspects of your life, you need to actively seek humor. Don't passively wait for random circumstances to make you laugh. Make a list of people and activities that you really enjoy and that make you laugh. Then get out your date book or calendar and schedule time to spend with those people or do those activities each week.

PEOPLE

_____ _____ _____

_____ _____ _____

ACTIVITIES

_____ _____ _____

_____ _____ _____

_____ _____ _____

_____ _____ _____

_____ _____ _____

Make your own laughter! It's good for you. Authors Faelten and Diamond have a wonderful suggestion for injecting humor into your life. Make a *"humor first-aid kit"* for yourself. Fill a shoe box with clippings from your favorite comic strips, funny magazine articles and pictures, humorous snapshots of friends or family, comedy cassette tapes, noisemakers, and funny disguises. Keep one humor first-aid kit at work and one at home. When your attitude begins to take a turn for the negative during the day, get some first-aid! Laugh, laugh, laugh and life will become a much more pleasant experience.

- THE CHAPTER IN BRIEF -

* A good sense of humor is essential to a healthy life.
* Laughter increases endorphins which ease the pain and help
   the body's resistance to disease.
* Laughter is fun and it's free.
* Learn to laugh at yourself.
* Make yourself a humor first-aid kit.

THREE

HOW YOU CAN AFFECT TEAM OR GROUP ATTITUDE

GROUP ATTITUDES

ave you ever heard phrases like, "That was an ugly crowd," "What a nice group of people," "They were a tough panel," "Congress is slow and ineffective," and "That team plays smart ball"? Each phrase refers to the personality and attitude of a group of people. *When a group or team gets together for a specific purpose, it tends to take on a group personality.* Ask any high-school teacher how different one group of students can be from the next. It's important to realize that when you are in a group or team, while you are still an individual, you have also become part of a separate entity. And that entity has unique character-istics and attitudes just like you do as an individual.

GROUP PERSONALITY

Make a list of groups, teams, etc., in which you are involved. Below each group, write down characteristics and attitude traits that describe it as a unit.

1. _____   2. _____

3. _____   4. _____

If you are a part of a group, team, committee, panel, club, or special task force, you should be aware of group dynamics and how you can influence them. It's a foregone conclusion that for the group to be successful in its task, it must have a positive attitude. You will never be able to control the attitudes of each group member. But there are specific ways that you can influence a group's *overall attitude*. The easiest way is to start with your own attitude. If you have a dynamic, positive attitude about the group and its purpose, your enthusiasm will spread to other members. *Attitudes, good and bad, can be very infectious*. So be sure to make an Attitude Check prior to each group meeting. Then help promote those positive feelings which will make the group successful at its task.

There are five ways that you can help ensure your group will have a positive, winning attitude about its purpose. First, *encourage a strong sense of group identity*. Assume the responsibility for keeping the group focused on the task. Encourage members to leave their outside problems and individual mind-sets out of group meetings. Avoid the politics that often plague a group situation. Don't take sides with one group member against another. These things only weaken the group's effectiveness. Always use terms like we, us, and our when speaking. Avoid using personal pronouns.

Another way to mold the group's positive attitude is to *make sure the group's ultimate goals are clear from the beginning*. You know how strong a team can become when everyone is focused on a clear, common goal. With some groups, goal-setting will be easier than with others. For instance, if you're on a sports team the goal is almost always to win the championship. Most groups at work are usually formed for very specific goals like increasing sales or improving department efficiency. But if you are involved with a group or organization which has no clearly stated goals, try to encourage your co-members to write down their goals so that you all know exactly what to focus on. Be specific when writing the goals and make sure to use active words like the ones in the example below.

EXAMPLE- Which group would you be more excited about? The group whose stated goal is to "Help improve the city" or the group whose goal is to, "Beautify the downtown area, provide adequate housing for the homeless, and stimulate lucrative tourism in the business district." A group whose members are focused on specific, active goals will have a positive attitude about itself.

The third way to maintain positive group attitude is a concept that we've already touched upon. *A group must have clear communication between its members*. If we use the analogy that a group is a living entity, what would happen if there were no communication between its parts? What if your brain didn't communicate clearly with your hands and feet? You wouldn't get anywhere. If you happened to step on a nail, you'd never know it. A group is the same way. Clear channels of communication must always be open for *every member of a group*.

The fourth way you can influence the attitude of a group is to know your role. In some groups, every member has the same role and generally does the same task. But in most groups, each member is expected to perform a different function. In the same way that the group's goals must be clear, each member's individual goals must be clear. For the group to succeed, *each member must know and accomplish his or her assignment or job responsibility*. Avoid infringing on other members' roles unless they ask for help.

EXAMPLE - Julia and Laura have been members of the Women's Circle for over two years. Ever since the first meeting, when she had volunteered, Julia had recorded the minutes. She wasn't the official secretary for the group, but she performed that function. One winter Julia caught pneumonia and missed several meetings. In her absence, Laura recorded the group's minutes. When Julia recovered and returned for the group's meeting, she sat down and began to take out her note pad. Laura saw this and said, "Don't you worry about that Julia. I'd be happy to record the minutes for you. This is your first meeting back with us so you just relax." Julia reluctantly put her pad away. At the next meeting, the same thing happened. Gradually, Laura had unwittingly usurped Julia's "job." Two weeks later, Julia began missing the meetings. The Women's Circle assumed she had become sick again.

In this example, what the group didn't realize was that Julia no longer felt needed and so dropped out. Taking minutes was not her official assignment, but she enjoyed doing it and felt it was her contribution to the group's success. Laura quite unmaliciously stole Julia's role in the group. So when participating in a group, be excited and positive about your role, but be sensitive to the roles of other members.

Finally, if you have any control over the actual make-up of the group, you must know who to choose and why. Leaders and bosses aren't successful because of their administrative skills alone. They are also successful by virtue of the people they choose to surround themselves with. When a leader has to put together a team for a specific purpose, he doesn't choose eight other leaders. He doesn't choose eight "idea" people. He doesn't choose eight efficiency experts. He doesn't people his group entirely with *any* single personality type. *The best teams and groups have perfect balance*. They are a unique blend of every personality type. If your group has several people who have the same personality type, they will tend to have confrontational relationships. If your group has several people with the same skill, they will find themselves vying for the same tasks and responsibilities within the group.

If you have the task of putting together a team for a project, be careful who you select. Don't choose your friends just because they are friends. Don't choose specific co-workers just because they are hard workers...*unless their specific skill or personality type is essential for your group*. Choosing the right team members will ensure a positive group attitude focused on success.

- THE CHAPTER IN BRIEF -

* Groups have characteristics and attitudes just as individuals do.
* Positive and negative attitudes can be infectious.
* Encouraging a strong sense of group identity, boosts group attitude.
* Set clear goals for the group from the beginning.
* Establish clear channels of communication.
* Every member must be clear on what his or her role is within the group so individuals' attitudes will be supportive.
* Choose a group with the proper balance of personality types and specific skills.

CONCLUSION

Attitude can mean everything! How you respond to what life offers you is a choice only you can make. Take time to consider who you are and what you want to accomplish in life. Take control of your attitude, set goals, use the power of positive thinking to overcome obstacles. This quote by Mary Kay Ash, president of Mary Kay Cosmetics, Inc., best captures the philosopy of positive attitude:

> "Aerodynamically the bumble bee shouldn't
> be able to fly, but the bumble bee doesn't
> know it so it goes on flying anyway."

You have the power to choose your own attitude and affect your life, so make the choice today!

BIBLIOGRAPHY

Adler, Mortimer J. How to Speak, How to Listen. New York: Macmillan, Co., 1983.

Ellis, Albert. How to Stubbornly Refuse to Make Yourself Miserable About Anything, Yes Anything. New York: Carol Publishing Group, 1990.

Faelton, Sharon, and David Diamond. Take Control of Your Life. Emmaus, PA: Rodale Press, 1988.

Frank, Milo O. How to Get Your Point Across in 30 Seconds Or Less. New York: Pocket, 1986.

Greenberg, Herbert M. Coping With Job Stress. New York: Prentice-Hall, 1986.

Handley, Robert. Anxiety and Panic Attacks. New York: Random House, 1985.

_____. The Life Plus Program for Getting Unstuck. New York: Random House, 1989.

Hanson, Peter G., M.D. The Joy of Stress. Kansas City, MO: Andrews, McMeel & Parker, 1985.

Helmstetter, Shad, Ph.D. The Self-Talk Solution. New York: Simon & Schuster, 1989.

_____. What to Say When You Talk to Yourself. New York: Simon & Schuster, 1982.

Jeffers, Susan, Ph.D. Feel the Fear and Do It Anyway. New York: Random House, 1987.

McQuade, Walter, and Ann Aikman. Stress. New York: Simon & Schuster, 1974.

Matthews, Andrew. Being Happy: A Handbook to Greater Confidence and Security. Los Angeles: Price Stern Sloan, Inc., 1988.

Nathan, Ronald G., Ph.D., et al. The Doctor's Guide to Instant Stress Relief. New York: Random House, 1987.

Peale, Norman Vincent. Positive Imaging: The Powerful Way to Change Your Life. New York: Fawcett-Crest, 1982.

Raber, Merrill F., M.S.W., Ph.D., and George Dyck, M.D. <u>Mental Fitness</u>. Los Altos, CA: Crisp Publications, 1987.

Waitley, Denis. <u>Being the Best</u>. New York: Simon & Schuster, 1987.

_____. <u>Joy of Working</u>. New York: Simon & Schuster, 1987.

Winter, Richard E. <u>Coping with Executive Stress</u>. New York: McGraw-Hill 1983.

NOTES

NOTES

NOTES

NOTES

NOTES

NOTES